PEARLS
Of the Sorrowful Nights

ONYEAMAI MARTIN

DEDICATION

To the Almighty

CONTENTS

Contents

ACKNOWLEDGMENTS

I acknowledge the nights when I battled the pain

I acknowledge the victories

I acknowledge you who will see the true texts

PEARLS OF THE SORROWFUL NIGHT

Night calls, owls sing
my soul bleeds of brazen pain
The tales deepen, calamity heightened
In my agony, I lost my presence
Found in a space bought in lonely coins
Deep thoughts of my present state
Dropped the beauty
The   pearls   of   the   nights   Sans   bliss

MY SHOOTING STAR

How can I take it off?
How can I scribble it out?
When the times, face and moments
Are now flashes of memory in my head.

Ah! Bullet!
A life you did not make.
My heart is filled with pain
I hope you can now eat what you killed?

I wish I can script all my feelings in a tab
Or shred my heart on a slab to get u back
Like the dragon's breath of a thousand-year folk tale.
Hero of Love!
My shooting star

O silent sleeping shed
Why did you let her in?
What was her sin.
That cannot be overlooked.
Why is there so much suffering
At the end, it is still sleep in a silent shed.

O eater of lost soul
Please give us back this one
And tell us the cost
When will you stop this trade of yours
And return my shooting star

How can I write it all
Why are we part of this game
Why did we come to this theatre
When we were just born to die
Why my shooting Star

O shooting star
Pay me one last visit
Please give me one last smile
Even if it is a frown
I will make every second count.

An Ode to a fallen Star
REQUIESCAT IN PACE!

MEAN-DMEE

Mean-dmee once said to me
Until you break it off
You cannot take it up
I failed to realize "it off"
Until is saw "me fall"
I tend to speak more about myself
Cos, I have come this road a lot
The emotions from the pain it wrought

Mean-dmee once said to me
Find yourself and the world will follow
"Eye" does not mean you see
I did not know this story.
Until I lost the glory
Now I see things clearly
Because a man once blind knows the pain
And how deep this dark can stain

Build your mind and leave it there
Someday you will learn the world is not fair
When all these friends are not there
At least you will have someone to tell
When you have built a man in there
Mean-dmee once said to me
At the two edges of life, you must rely on someone else
But at the center must be a strong me.

COLD SILENT MUD

He had ended his life in its prime.
A young, lively child with style
He has eaten his life in time.
All because he has followed a world so wild.
He has believed in a man so vile.
Instead of holding strong to his God,
Now he has gone to bed in a basket.
Beneath this cold, silent mud.

WORDS OF MY HEART

The words of my heart may not be wise.
But I have taken it for real.
Because when this world of deceit
Will strike you to your feet,
It is only his words
That will get you off the heat
The words of my heart may not be nice
But I will respect it all the same
Because even when the world may not be nice
It will console your heavy sighs
And gather your dripping eyes
To break the man off the boy
The words of my heart may not give a hug
Because I have been stabbed many times
By harmless hugs
The fabric of man is wicked
Aye! Its wickedness consoles me
Hence, my curiosity is served.

BLEEDING HEART

Heavy hearts are like heavy clouds
They need to let go some rain, to be free again
To let go of this pain, I must free this rain.
Just to feel again.

Bleeding hearts are like acid clouds
They peel the flesh out of healthy grounds.
Despite this pain, I can think again.
So, to preach to a craving heart.

Despise your pain, I call it gain.
Because through the thorns I see the rose.
So, pick the pearls let the tears.
Close your eyes and love again.

Love and hate are but the same.
With a thin line to separate.
With a broken heart, you tend to hate.
But be strong my love and love again.

I feel great pain, I cannot think straight.
Isn't the way I saw it ends
My heart so thick, eyes are blur.
Sorrow for less, love again.

NOT NO MORE

From a bleeding heart,
Is a hurting song.
From a weeping eye,
Are lightning sparks.
From a gentle heart,
Is a humble call.
This loyal one,
Is calm no more.

A sorrowful song,
From a burning heart.
A gentle lamb
Constantly slaughtered.
Now the gates are locked.
Everyone shut out.
Am not loving no more.
Not no more!

OVERFLOWING THOUGHT

Your pacing thoughts
Are opening doors
My ailing heart
Is healing not
Sobering eyes
Can make creative lines
A bleeding tongue
Can cause unending burns
Certain bonds
Are like missing songs
A fuming heart
Is like falling Rocks
And now my thoughts
The brim can hold no more

ILLUMINATED BY THOUGHT

I have been drawing
The lines are falling
Waiting for the one who is calling
To fill the lining
The night is boring
The picture of a future-blurry

I have been thinking
The mind is running
Does anyone deserve this mourning
Soldiers of the Dark Drumming
When will he reach his calling
True beauty is like a purpose-hidden

My heart is racing
Reaching for one deserving.
Melting through the night,
That is stormy.
Native wordings.
the night is humming.
Our ghosts are calling
Merrily hauling
Scornful   and   loving

WHISTLING PAST AN ILLUSION

The skies are dull
Yet can absorb light and reflect beauty
The heart is flesh
But can be as hard as rock
Stories are told
But the ones we tell ourselves are true
Only because they are made true by us

My heart is restless
All because of the things I see
Every picture whisper a story
Yours just told me one.
A tale of you
A reflection of your innermost self
Pain and love can be the same word.

The heart of man is transparent
Because it was only made of fibre
Blood can make it opaque
An illusion of what there be
Cast your gaze, you might see you in mine
Only take care, it might be a hallucination
The game of truth has begun

They call it trust
I say it is a fool's word.
Like love it only make us weak.
Expectations is an indicator of betrayal.
Love and trust go hand in hand
So, I call it a mine field for pain
Listen with your mind, it might be saying something

I have grown pass this phase
So I sit in wait for you to strike
And let you see the truth.

That in all your wisdom, it is folly
Your absolute ingenuity is a waste of time
Let you understand that you are just an illusion
All I will do is whistle pass the illusion

IF HURT BE A THEME, WHERE THEN IS LOVE?

Mother O Mother!
Our soil destroyed by the infertility of the old lady.
Who in menopause, has refused to leave the bed of the groom.
For this young bride to use the loom!

Mother O Mother!
Hundred years and still counting!
The blame game on and unending.
'The whites left us no heritage at independence!'.

Mother O Mother!
Let the patriots converge.
Let us look for a future for dying mama.
Lest she dies and we bury her in silence forever.

Mother O Mother!
Our land so rich, the envy of all nations.
Our beauty in our diversity.
Has now become a thorn, catalyzing our divisibility.

I pledge to Nigeria my country.
To be faithful loyal and honest.
To serve Nigeria with all my strength.
Is now like a rhyme, in the mouth of an infant.

Mother O Mother!
Where then is the luster we used in gaining dependence?
1st October Nine tea six tea, we danced and feasted.
We 6th July nine things 67 converged again for our destruction.

Mother O Mother!
Tribulation upon tribulation.
Deceit upon deceit, the conspiracy continues.
When then shall we come together to reap independence?

Mother O Mother!
Green and white is the colour.
A black nation with white background.
Total deceit! Green, Black and Red is the true colour.

Mother O Mother!
Bitterness, Religion, Terrorism, Tribalism, Nepotism, Corruption,
Greed no long suffering!
The Nigerian wealth is now a national cake.
Even the cursed and dying are in the queue for a bite.

O youths, you who are true to a fault!
Come together with thine thoughts.
Let us build our nation to a fort.
Not even to be dented by a dot.

FEBUARY'S FORTH-INN

A land once polished by green.
Polished in fragrance unaltered.
A soil known for unwavering calm.
Now I hear two suns have risen in one sky.
The northern sun proposes the southern oppose.
The southern sun accepts, and refusal is the norths.
A land where one sun has scorched us so hard.
And our fear comes to book.
Is now threatened by a duo.
A duo in a duet,
A threat to our survival.
Our wealth, unrest.

The drums are beating up.
I hear the drummers are unwavering.
Their solidarity and loyalty unflinching.
The drums of war are beating.
 February, feign-boar-tarry.

Your fourth-inn has promised to crush.
Like a boa to its prey, I fear your sight.
How can we avoid this albatross tale foreseen.
The two suns rise my kin bleed.
This soil graced with the allure of gold.
Now is Chanting war!
This same pride we share,
 Is now used to brew the weapons of our demise.

Weeds of the North weep,
In fear of the flame.
Southern weeds, the axe!
And the soil unrest.
Relax friend! The word I hear.
How can I, when even the clouds nearest the sun are set for flight.
Their sons at large.

Here is me, my father with me.
So is you, and your father with you.
Call me a harbinger of doom.
Prophet doom if you wish.
But this pill called truth, is bitter not sweet.
So, Arise, o compatriot.
Your mothers call obey
Your native land to protect.
Chase blood sucking demons away.
This labour of our hero's past.
Shall never be in vain.
So, serve with heart and might.
Our nation bound in freedom, peace, and unity.

ALLE! A BECKON TO SHARE MY FEELINGS

Alle! The sound and stench that gets my heart beating.
A rhythm I didn't know of its existing.
At your thought I'm drowned in an ocean of fantasy.
FANTA-SEE! The sight that makes the children happy.
"ALLE, I FANTA-SEE YOU!"
I wake up with fear and sadness. I never see!
The Fear that soon, I'm about to lose you.
And Sadness of my fate after I see this.

 She, like you radiate so much beauty.
A beauty with weight but description never seen.
Her smile is a portion for making love charms.
Her frown, the talisman for chasing the devil.
Her colour, as bright and accommodating as the morning clouds.
That weather that no one prays to miss.
Her tears, a pail that empties my heart with sadness.
The sadness that can put a man in madness.
Her skin, as soft as the morning breeze.
Oh! I see why mother earth is called a mother.

  Alle, I am in tears because you don't understand how I feel.
My love for you is never rewarded.
I strive to please; instead of bliss, the heat, I feel.
Alle, my heart is bitter, thus I write.
To empty my heart with a pen on paper.
Hoping someday, you will read this letter.
Mama! Alle has eaten me mental.

 To you who too have been punished by love.
Mourn with me 'cos you feel my torment.
And so, I feel, true love, she, never deserving.
Here I drop this pen as my feeling really I cannot express!

VOICE OF THE HEART

I saw the light fade before my eyes,
Sons of light lose their sight
Somewhere too blue a place.
I saw children flying,
I saw bullets dying.

I heard of wars against the sons of light.
I heard "No more Tutsi"
I heard "No more Hutu"
I saw the looters turn ancient Bini kingdom to ruins.
I saw walking woods vomiting fire; its power, men depend on

Man, not satisfied with the rate of falling corpse,
Awoke the stones of death, and virtually wiped out his habitat.
Innocent blood cry out of Hiroshima
saying "where is justice"
Behold the skies were silent, our sky of justice.

The cloud now has giving in to the pressure of the sun,
All because of man's hunger
Our world run out of time
As the sun threatening to dry up the waters & lands

"Man has virtually killed all his predator and has started killing himself"

THIS THOUGHT!

I have this drawing in my heart.
Its shape, I cannot tell
Square? No! Cube? No!
But it tells me of my failing love.
So irregular and unkempt with sides like an orchard unpruned.
Ailing thoughts!
Its texture seems smooth but it's really rough.
So much deceit, drawing up my fury.
But tell me. Is love really not deceitful?
Isn't love tardy, rough and unkempt?

For you who had just entered the race,
Be wary lest the last of your treasure be beating to pulp.
The drumming that gives you ecstasy. Like ESTHER SEE!
That drowns you in a utopia, designed for you even out of your phobia.
That rhythm that you always want to repeat.
The rhymes, I always want to listen.
The lyrics, manuals of your very defeat. Early defeat!

Oh! Feel this drumming in your heart as I do.
Has love captured me again? TABOO!
Shh! Listen so you can play it back to me.
So, I can see your face in the song.
Flow with the melody.
Dance to the symphony.

The very sun that sings a song.
You that illuminates the land where I belong.
Your care, and presence, oh your voice, I long!
The love my grandma calls imai-krokozim.
Trying to mimic the word microcosm.
Micro-cosy, micro-cosmic. Yes, micro but the effects are costly.
That very touch that kills my sense, my tonic.

Hope you feel like me now?
Lying in a sea of rubies, adorned with roses.
My sun, my song, my love, my long!
All thoughts!

AGYMANAK...A TRIBUTE TO A FALLEN HERO!

Lira! Nira! Zira!
The sound that reminds me that a hero has fallen.
And still my trumpet of tribute, silent.
Float away in thoughts.
I see his figure, unshaken.
My professor, the great Iroko, has fallen.
One whose star shone bright on the night skies.
And inspired me to linger.
My honorable whose hairs stand firm in coordination.
A governor amongst governors.
One who they that now mourn his exit,
Once plotted his diminish.
Hypocrites in friendly apparel.
Wolves on sheep skin.
A man who sees great of the people he serves.
And sees a counsellor in me.

I salute you great prof.
Because you have taken the exeat,
To live the life of endless end.
My heart bleeds to recall how empty this life is.
I call this thank you, cause after the pain comes thanks.
After birth comes thanks.
I hear in Egypt, there is life after death
In death I know you will smile.
As your suit has shone as the sun.
And now like the phoenix, thy birth is come.
Until the fire comes, your rebirth and newness is naught.
Aye prof! My ink, your tale, cannot stop talking.
A king gone to return with power.
And so, I expect your enthronement great one.
Requiescat in pace...my brother and friend.

4 late hon. Richard Akpobulokemi.

OH, DRACONIAN DEVIL O LAME SAINT

Though in our fellowship we bind to the dogmas of darkness.
Our karma lay aside a table from whence we shalst return.
Yet again to drink and merry in our very penance.

In our own inclination
of our own self will we chose our path,
Of life? of death? in passion we decide.
Yet is the pain of our memories, a drum unsettled.
Do we then judge ye holy yet dreadful one; our past on our very future.
That the brick we bear hinder the truth we fear.
That man was made to be punished, a sport for his deity.

For on the day shalst I speak in wrath.
Of the way man's heart wickedness hath wrought.
That in that day would mellow I be not; till man's all debt be paid.

Oh, Beast of Comfort, of Death
Of the peace that kills, of the riches of pain.
Spare oh Angel of Light, our frailty, to the Dark hast drawn us.

As to wanton Boys, are we to the gods...They Kill us for their Sport – Williams Shakespeare

WHAT WE SHARE

Born off the crucible
He had his own share visible.
The pain, times we bled were tangible.
The times when I never had been reasonable.
Yet we shared this bond you were credible.
The piece is for the friend who stood within the ambient of reach
when life cut the string.

I have no problems with the scars…
My only scare is story they tell.
Of the times we bled yet in vain
Of our hopes without gain
When our passion was our bane
Of a rose sans thorn
Yet we met a Bush of thorns
And when we get here?
We know it is rare.
What we share.

Touch my heart and feel its burns.
The frustration you carry lays me bare.
The gas that runs the engine may be fear.
But dear, we would never go back there.
I have learnt from the best to steer.
May never trust the mellow seas or the albatross.
And even as I speak, I see no hill
Or the hope of a glorious shore.

Yet on faith I hold so firm
That what we share will bring us there
At the end we wage this war
And our shoulder will take it all
Like the 300 of legend Leonidas
We will take them all.
We should take them all
Standing tall.

UGLY PAST

Touched by the sun
I Think I can feel the burn
Reminiscing might be fun
Until you hit this bump
An Ugly past.

Hunted by your beasts
Taunted to fall.
The spirits of your evils gone,
Haunts the hall.
I feel the silent call
And the bellowing drums.
Calling for its turn.

Rage, hate, stakes and blood.
All products of the run.
Their Calls knocking you up.
Knuckles shiver
Silent thoughts
Raging bump
Flowing sweats
Going numb
Silent perspirations
As your beasts come calling
Echoing halls
Winding screams
Wild shatters
No sun.

love is death...

Like a candle lit, it burns so hard, fueled by wax even as it dies slowly

The nights come
Darkness unending
The stakes call
Silence unending
Yet mind voices blaring.
Cannot hear myself
I am feeling scared
Picked up a rifle
But am I ending here?

Who will tell the stories
Of our ugly past
Who will cure the cancer
Of our erring acts
Who will preach the message
Of the stories there
Who but a prophet
Who had once been there.
Who will help the children
Who will save them
Who will teach the people
Of the unending horror
Of the echoing nights
Of an ugly past.

ECHOES OF THE UNSPOKEN SONG

Beaten by an overlaboured thought.
An overburdened heart,
Stress he bought
I am this, I am that,
I know I am great yet failed.
The song of my head bellows on
Deafening the acting me.
And now while I failed,
All there is, is an unspoken song.

No matter what beauty tells you that you have
Always know that it is ephemeral
And when it fades away
Like the ashes fade away
With the silent wind
Then will you understand
The veracity of a lying Tongue
You have been conned by Youth!

Teach me to fear
Not my enemies
But the consequences of my unweighted actions.
Teach me to fight
Not my conscience
But the voice of intimidation from an oppressive heart.
Help me to speak
Not for myself
But for the mouth that has lost its voice
That I may fight
For what is right
And be not a wall
To my neighbor's light!

This song is for the man
Who works so hard
In thought, in words
Over bloated pride
Over blown consciousness
Sans Work?
An unspoken song…all imagination.

LOVE UNKIND

How can I describe you
A million tales in one
Laden beneath the elegance of a masterpiece.
The colour and culture of extravagance.
A beauty beyond letters.
Tale beyond speech.

How will I measure you?
Colours sans serif
Beauty beyond reason
And when my heart drop in,
Deceit beyond measure
Uncertainty taints my pleasure,
Fear spikes my heart.
The picture of a rose ☐ My deceit!

Neither once nor twice or thrice
You try to be strong
You fight your echoing doubts
Wake up to your fears
Yet the circle continues to stare
You hear elm say
Take the bull by the horn
Be a man and be in control
What happens when the bull of my love is without horns
Where will I find the man when I have lost his control.
Or When I embrace this bitterness Of Love unkind!

98 THAT JUNE ATE (8)

(I want to tell you a story about 98, that June Ate)

On this evening of 98
Something happened I was to hate
Was it France 98?
Or an event of a ruler slayed
He was an only child, but it was his fate
I heard Silence speak
 And then the eruption "hurray!!!"
It was him; calamity evacuates.
We won, he took the bait

What would I have told 7 of the 8
That the great dictator you met is late.
And still the 8 headed hydra again surfaces
To wake us up to the dreams we hate.
For 12 years he begged to stay
His words were to raise the stakes
That change is here to stay
And now we are back in chains and pains
Awaiting 98 that June ate.

SORO SOKE

We are a woke generation
Awakened by our Hunger for justice
We deserve to live
Yes, the leaders of tomorrow should live to see tomorrow.

Generations before us slept
Waiting for a better Nigeria
Now we here stagnant
We here stunted, brutalized, impoverished
And our neck under the knee

Soro Soke! We must!
Its ok! No, it's not!
We cannot stay in pain whilst we smile
Like its, ok?
Soro soke for the one who was shot yet denied justice.
The child, beaten yet asked not to cry.
The mothers who must bear a child
And mourn him before his prime.
The father who is forced to pick up his dead son from the river of
bodies.

Soro soke for the girl Tina
Her candle was thinned out and cut
By the same men we empowered with the gun
Soro soke! Against the system that stands and watch us die
While they move around our streets with their bullion vans
Not anymore!
Soro soke! For ishaq and Henry
Whose only crime was to say enough is enough!

Soro soke!
To the martyrs of this revival
Men and women whose lives are the sacrifices of our liberation.
Soro soke!
To the victims of this struggle
Who have lived their live

Bearing the trauma of their encounter.

Soro Soke! to a failed System.
The political SARS
To the man called to represent us yet serves himself.
To the man whose renumeration is enough to feed his community.
Whose legislation is for the elites
And the voice of the street is mere gossip.
Soro soke!
As we raise our glass
To the New Nigeria
A woke Generation!

Now the government be taking our lives too?
We thought all they do be take our lives for granted.
Inflict pain and hardship on the masses.
Enrich themselves and impoverish the armless.
Discredit a righteous struggle.
Now they drink our bloods too?
Shame on our leaders!
They take our mandate and gift us the casket.
Take our votes and all they give us is violence.
Soro Soke till no one be silent.
Till death and the gunshots inspire us.
Soro Soke cos that is the only choice not quiet

THE BANQUET 21

For 20 She bled
A naïve soul Cursed to hell
She dived without care
Forced to love without fear
A fool she was to them.

For 20 she loved so dear
Her heart she lent and shared
20 times she felt the blade
As pain became her fate
Like Caesar, Brutus dealt the death

She bled for 20
The blade and the sore she bore
Hoping that love will ease her pain
A cheap sedative it was
Only Wore off before it's born.

For 20 she tended her wounds
Like a soldier would do after a battle.
At ease for 21 is a banquet
Like victors we feast in scores

She loved so hard her 20
Paid the price for love
Yet came back with pain
Hear, 21 would be different

And the gates shall 21 shut
So come 20 let's clear the tables now
For the feast is only ready for a few
For 21 is a banquet

THE AUDACITY OF THE SHAMED

This is me in my story
At the end of the kiln is a kin
Suffering tribalism, sexism, racism all "is isms"
What is every people's story without the shamed

This is me in my story
inferiority, my sole sorority
berated for my size, and look, the abs-less scorn
Less delight, undelectable, the public's laughingstock

This is me, in my story
Driven away by my peers
My looks incoherent with their utopia
Driven aback, shelled off the spotlight

This is me, in my story
Told only abs can make you loved
What audacity have you to even feel free
Such fatty, plumpy, pork

This is me in my story
Used and shamed, I hid from fame
Forced to go under the scalpel, or take the knife
But when my light dims, fake lovers assemble

The is me hoping I can tell this story
Of the struggle we face, the battles to fit-in
Needless adventure, for someone so Special
Why crave the spotlight when you are the spotlight

This is me, standing tall
Often scared to take off the toppings
The fear of being the ridicule
Lost confidence, expected the world to give it back

Take the spot, challenge status-quo
Make a statement, dare the talkers
Find your beauty, make it count
Seize the spot, make bold your weakness
That is the audacity of the shamed

STALE

I hope the night brings you peace
That the morning meets you in bliss
I crave the light that shine deep
That your love flows still
Through thick, through thin to find me

Gentle wind blows steep
I hope that meets you still
Where our hearts once beats
A certain hill sans end
A gentle sail wrought still

FROZEN PAIN

Heart bleeds
Burnt by the frost
Of this cold love
tongues of Deceit, hurt, bitterness
Honeycomb coats
Insecurity calls
My trust is lost
Cold nights colder
Tears drizzling
till my heart is frozen
The craft of a heartless beast
My misplaced feelings
Betrayed by my own heart Now caged
Will never speaks again as it dies of frozen pain

SOON

It is about time, I know
Once Bent by the swirling wind
Now Shaped to perfection
A brew only for legends
have Crossed the hottest edifices
A product of the kiln
Born of the furnace
made to stand with the stars
where She belongs
Excellence imperfect before her
Virtue stands no chance
She is the empress
A raging army adores
Who find such precious in time
The sands of time she shapes
Our star is enthroned
Curves of beauty every smile adorns
Royalty behooves, every step illuminates
A queen and sire
Never a shy to style
And soon, a star, she is.

LONE STAR

How do I speak of ghosts and teary nights
Of tales that hurt,
events that haunt
sans confident {French}
How do I say this
O world, I am all alone.
The life of a lone star

How do I say these words
make sense of my pain,
write of this hurt or find my consolation
How do I say I cannot love
or I live in fear of hurt unhealed
or the scars they create
How do I tell the tale when no one cares

who will I tell of a lone star
at the edge of the sky
of this loving soul who cannot share
of a heart frost bitten in times past
who shares the pain
of a wanderer star
afraid of another scar

ABOUT THE POET

A lonely soul once spoke these words, a lover's heart once shredded.
A scared patriot afraid of what his world would be.
A lover of deep secrets

-Martin D Leo